NO KIDDING!

MoNsTeR and CREEPY-CRAWLY Jokes, Riddles, and Games

Rachel Eagen

Crabtree Publishing Company
www.crabtreebooks.com

Crabtree Publishing Company
www.crabtreebooks.com

Author: Rachel Eagen

Editorial Director: Ellen Rodger

Art Director: Rosie Gowsell Pattison

Editor: Petrice Custance

Proofreader: Janine Deschenes

Prepress technician: Margaret Amy Salter

Print and production coordinator: Katherine Berti

Production coordinated by Plan B Book Packagers

Photographs:
Cover and title page: Maryna Ivanova/Shutterstock; p.2: Egg Design/Shutterstock; p.3: Lightspring/Shutterstock; p.4 (UPLE): Abeadev/Shutterstock; p.4: (LOLE): Waldru/Shutterstock; p.5 (UP): Lek Changply/Shutterstock; p.5 (LOLE): Albert Ziganshin/Shutterstock; p.6 (LOLE): Baimieng/Shutterstock; p.6 (LORT): Anneka/Shutterstock; p.7 (LOLE): Jane 0606/Shutterstock; p. 7 (UPRT): Sarawut Padungkwan/Shutterstock; p.8 (LOLE): Nito/Shutterstock; p.8 (LORT): Richard Peterson/Shutterstock; p. 9 (UPRT): Stamatoyoshi/Shutterstock; p.9 (LORT): Albert Ziganshin/Shutterstock; p. 10 (LOLE): Maridav/Shutterstock; p.10 (MIDRT): Luca Montevecchi/Shutterstock; p.11 (UPLE): Memo Angeles/Shutterstock; p.11 (LOLE): Roxana Bashyrova/Shutterstock; p. 12: Willee Cole Photography/Shutterstock; p.13 (MIDLE): Fixer 00/Shutterstock; p.13 (UPRT): Alexander Raths/Shutterstock; p.14 (LOLE): Real Illusion/Shutterstock; p.14(MIDRT): Real Illusion/Shutterstock; p.14 (LORT): Real Illusion/Shutterstock; p.15 (UPLE): Elenarts/Shutterstock; p.15 (UPRT): Valentina Razumova/Shutterstock; p.16: Vasin Srethaphakdi/Shutterstock; p.17(LOLE): Lightspring/Shutterstock; p.17 (UPRT): Ilya Andriyanov/Shutterstock; p.18 (LOLE): Anthony Paul Taylor/Shutterstock, p.18 (LORT): Oleg Belov/Shutterstock; p.8 (LORT): John Foto 18/Shutterstock; p.19 (MIDLE): Blambca/Shutterstock; p.19 (UPRT): Production Perig/Shutterstock; p.20 (UPRT): Malchev/Shutterstock; p.20 (LORT): Valentina S./Shutterstock; p.21(UPLE): Albert Ziganshin/Shutterstock; p. 21 (UPRT): No Brand 121876/Shutterstock; p.22 (LORT): Albert Ziganshin/Shutterstock; p.22 (LOLE): IvanNikulin/Shutterstock; p.22 (LORT): IvanNikulin/Shutterstock; p.23 (UP): Thomas Klee/Shutterstock; p.23 (UPRT): Elisanth/Shutterstock; p.23(LOLE): Rudall 30/Shutterstock; p.24: Nicescene; p.25 (UP): Christina Richards/Shutterstock; p.25(LOLE): Ivan Nikulin/Shutterstock; p.26: Nito/Shutterstock; p.27 (UPLE): Albert Ziganshin/Shutterstock; p.27 (UPRT): Albert Ziganshin/Shutterstock; p.28: Albert Ziganshin/Shutterstock; p.29: Egg Design/Shutterstock; p.30: Egg Design/Shutterstock; p.31 (MIDLE): Elena Schweitzer/Shutterstock; p.31 (UPRT): Logan 81/Shutterstock

Library and Archives Canada Cataloguing in Publication

Eagan, Rachel, author
        Monster and creepy-crawly jokes, riddles, and games / Rachel Eagen.

(No kidding!)
Includes index.
Issued in print and electronic formats.
ISBN 978-0-7787-2389-9 (bound).--
ISBN 978-0-7787-2393-6 (paperback).--
ISBN 978-1-4271-1746-5 (html)

        1. Monsters--Juvenile humor. 2. Wit and humor, Juvenile. 3. Riddles, Juvenile. I. Title.

PN6231.M665R64 2016   jC818'.602   C2015-907479-7
                                                 C2015-907480-0

Library of Congress Cataloging-in-Publication Data

Names: Eagen, Rachel, 1979- author.
Title: Monster and creepy-crawly jokes, riddles, and games / Rachel Eagen.
Description: New York : Crabtree Publishing, [2016] | Series: No kidding! | Includes index. | Description based on print version record and CIP data provided by publisher; resource not viewed.
Identifiers: LCCN 2015050836 (print) | LCCN 2015049817 (ebook) | ISBN 9781427117465 (electronic HTML) | ISBN 9780778723899 (reinforced library binding : alk. paper) | ISBN 9780778723936 (pbk. : alk. paper)
Subjects: LCSH: Monsters--Juvenile humor. | Wit and humor, Juvenile. | Riddles, Juvenile.
Classification: LCC PN6231.M665 (print) | LCC PN6231.M665 E14 2016 (ebook) | DDC 818/.5402--dc21
LC record available at http://lccn.loc.gov/2015050836

Crabtree Publishing Company
www.crabtreebooks.com   1-800-387-7650

Printed in Canada/032016/EF20160210

Published in Canada
Crabtree Publishing
616 Welland Ave.
St. Catharines, Ontario
L2M 5V6

Published in the United States
Crabtree Publishing
PMB 59051
350 Fifth Avenue, 59th Floor
New York, New York 10118

Published in the United Kingdom
Crabtree Publishing
Maritime House
Basin Road North, Hove
BN41 1WR

Published in Australia
Crabtree Publishing
3 Charles Street
Coburg North
VIC, 3058

Contents

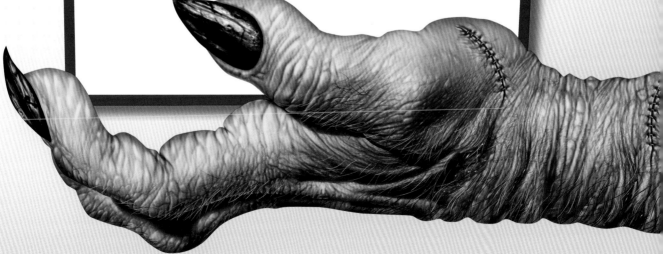

Chapter 1
Muahahaha

Why is it so fun to laugh?

Is it because laughter makes us feel happy? Or is it because we simply can't help it? And what kinds of things make us laugh? For some people it's watching something ridiculous, like when a little kid tries to walk around in adult shoes. For others, the right word said at the right time and place can make us bust a gut.

SCARY CAN BE FUNNY

A lot of people find scary things funny. That's right! Scary things such as giant spiders with fake hairy legs in a horror film. Why is this funny? Humor experts (yes, there are people who study things that are funny), think that we laugh at things that are threatening but also safe at the same time. It's a way of relieving stress. So, we might laugh at someone tripping over their shoelaces, but not if they were injured. We wouldn't find it funny that someone broke their nose after tripping over their shoelaces. It's not funny to laugh when someone is hurt.

To "bust a gut" is a slang term. It means to laugh so hard you hurt your stomach.

Q How do monsters like their eggs?

A Terrified! Yuk yuk yuk...

Q What kind of dog does Dracula have?

A A bloodhound! Get it? Muahahaha!

FUNNY BONE:
A cackle is a sharp, throaty laugh. It is often used in books and plays to describe a witch's nasty laughter.

LAUGHING SICKNESS?

Laughter can be contagious. No really, we mean it! In 1962, a school in Tanzania was closed down for a time during a laughter **epidemic**. It started with three students and spread like a virus throughout the school. Students could not stop laughing and nobody could get anything done. The laughter was called an epidemic. It was believed to have been caused by stress. The students could have easily cried or gotten sick, but their bodies and minds reacted with laughter instead.

HA HA HA HA HA HA!

I DIED LAUGHING!

We often use the phrase "I'm dying" when we are laughing really hard. But can people really die laughing? There have been some cases where a heart attack or stroke occurred after some hearty laughter, but those people are usually already in poor health. Laughter is actually thought to be very good for our health. At the very least, it makes us feel great!

DARK HUMOR

Dark humor is anything that pokes fun at serious, stressful, and frightening things. This includes jokes and comments made about war, death, and crime. It might seem odd, but comedy often follows tragedy. People sometimes need to relieve their pain by making fun of a situation they cannot change. You might have used your own form of dark humor when being punished by your parents for something you did wrong. If your punishment was to clean the bathroom for example, you might look at your dog and say "well at least I don't have to clean *your* toilet."

THIS MIGHT BE FAMILIAR...

Many well-known children's books and movies use dark humor. Nasty villains are often described as humorously ugly and not very smart. For example, in the children's book *The BFG* (The Big Friendly Giant) by Roald Dahl, a vegetable-eating giant teams with a girl who lives in a horrible orphanage. Together, they convince the Queen of England to imprison nine human-eating giants. The giants have names such as Meatdripper, Childchewer, Bloodbottler, and Fleshlumpeater. The names are scary sounding, but also funny!

Q

What do you call a fast-eating monster?

A A goblin.

FUNNY BONE:

To the ancient Greeks, the term humor did not mean funny. Instead, they believed the humors were four body fluids: blood, yellow bile, black bile, and phlegm. These humors were thought to control health. In "good humor" meant in good shape. Today, in good humor means being happy.

Chapter 2
Just Jokin'

There are many different types of jokes. Comedians, who are people who make their living being funny, often specialize in styles of humor. Despite jokes' differences, every joker knows that all good jokes follow a similar pattern.

ANATOMY OF A JOKE

Jokes have two basic parts. The **setup** tells you what you need to know to get, or understand, the joke. The **punch line** is the payoff, or the zinger that comes at the end. It's usually the punch line that makes people laugh. Here's a creepy-crawly example:

SETUP:
What kind of
wig can hear?

PUNCH LINE:
An earwig!

BUILD UP

Not all jokes are short and simple. Some jokes can take several minutes to tell. Longer jokes rely on buildup, which allows the joker to delay the punch line. When a joker is using buildup, he or she will add details to the joke, so that it sounds more like a story. Usually, buildup helps to make a joke even funnier. Stand-up comedians are experts at using buildup. They can often draw out a joke over a whole set, or part of an act or show. This can last half an hour or more. These sets are designed with several punch lines along the way. This gives the audience little payoffs that hold their attention. These payoffs also keep them happy and in their seats.

You don't want to bore your audience with overly long buildups.

8

Here's an example of a joke with buildup. See if you can find the setup and punch line:

A man walks into a doctor's office, holding his stomach.

"What's wrong?" asks the doctor.

The man shakes his head. "If I told you, you'd never believe me," he says.

"Come on, try me," says the doctor. "I've seen a lot of things in my day."

"Okay," says the man. "The thing is, there's a monster in my belly."

"A monster?" asks the doctor.

"Yes, a monster," says the man.

"How did it get in there?" asks the doctor.

"Well, I yawned and he just jumped right in."

The doctor frowns. "That is very serious," he says. "We're going to have to operate on you right away."

So the doctor gives the man some anesthetic and operates on the man. When the man wakes up, he sees the doctor standing beside the bed. He's holding onto a leash with a blue monster at the end of it.

"The operation was a success," says the doctor. "We found this monster in your belly. You must feel a lot better now."

"Not really," says the man. "The monster I swallowed was green."

Q

Why do mummies make good employees?

They get all wrapped up in their work.

A

9

WHAT'S MY LINE?

Think it's hard to remember a joke? Imagine taking to the stage without any jokes at all! That's what **improv** actors do. Improv comedians perform in groups. Together, they create skits, or short, humorous plays, without any preparation and with no scripted, or written, jokes. They are usually given just a sentence or two to get started. Sometimes, audiences give the actors a starting point, such as: *You're taking a walk in the woods when you think you see Bigfoot.* The performers will take the suggestion to begin the skit, but then take it in many wild and wacky directions.

Q What's green and sings?

A Elvis Parsley

WHAT A GAG!

Gags are jokes without words. They rely on physical tricks to make people laugh. Sometimes, gags are used to surprise people, so that they become the punch line. For example, try putting a sign that says "Wet Paint" on a park bench that's perfectly dry, and watch people avoid sitting on it all afternoon.

OH NO!

A whoopee cushion is a rubber cushion that makes the sound of a fart when someone sits on it. It is a type of gag joke.

MIMICKING FOR FUN

A **parody** is a joke that makes fun of something or someone through imitation. The trick is to exaggerate a well-known trait, or characteristic, of the person or thing being parodied. It can be dressing up as a celebrity or imitating how someone talks. Parodies can also be songs, poems, or videos.

Elvis Presley was a famous singer whom many performers like to parody.

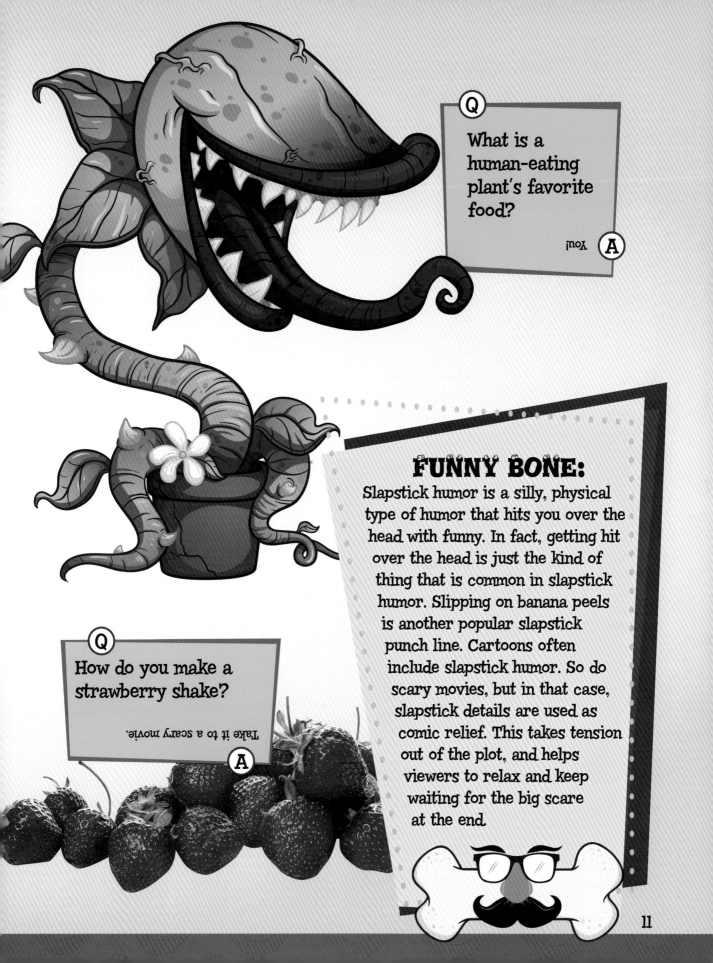

Q

What is a human-eating plant's favorite food?

A You!

Q

How do you make a strawberry shake?

A Take it to a scary movie.

FUNNY BONE:

Slapstick humor is a silly, physical type of humor that hits you over the head with funny. In fact, getting hit over the head is just the kind of thing that is common in slapstick humor. Slipping on banana peels is another popular slapstick punch line. Cartoons often include slapstick humor. So do scary movies, but in that case, slapstick details are used as comic relief. This takes tension out of the plot, and helps viewers to relax and keep waiting for the big scare at the end.

Chapter 3
The Culture of Humor

Humans first laughed to cope in stressful situations, such as an attack from a woolly mammoth. Talk about laughing in the face of danger! Today, **gelotologists**, or scientists who study laughter, believe that laughing is important to our social bonds. Laughing helps us to connect with others and shows that we feel safe among our friends.

AROUND THE WORLD

Laughter is one of the few things that all people around the world love to do. Humor can work as a common language that unites people, even when they don't share the same customs or language. But that doesn't mean that everyone finds the same things funny. This is especially true when jokes are translated from one language into another. For example, **puns** are word jokes with a double meaning. But when a pun is translated from one language into another, the joke usually has to be explained so much that it isn't funny anymore.

> **Q**
>
> What kind of monster loves to disco?
>
> The boogieman!
>
> **A**

TRICK OR TREAT!

So, why do we laugh, anyway? What makes something funny...funny? Scientists believe that it has a lot to do with the unexpected. That's because our brains naturally think in patterns that we can easily anticipate, such as: "If a big scary dog chases me, I'll run!" A joke presents something that you don't see coming, like when the big scary dog licks your face, or lies down at your feet and plays dead. Jokes are a bit like tricks that work as treats for your brain.

YUK YUK SCIENCE

You might think that laughter comes from your belly, but a good laugh actually starts in your head. When we hear a good joke, parts of our brain become very active, processing the words or events in the joke until we "get it." The brain then sends messages that stimulate a physical response, such as laughter. When we laugh, our body releases special chemicals called **endorphins**, whose job in our bodies is to make us feel happy!

Many people find clowns scary. It really isn't surprising, since clowns have exaggerated expressions and bright makeup that make them appear a little frightening.

HUMOR AND HEALTH

You may have heard the expression, "Laughter is the best medicine." It's true! Laughter is very good for our health. It increases the production of antibodies, which are substances that help us fight infection and illness. Laughing also helps to reduce stress, lower blood pressure, and generally make you feel better.

FUNNY BONE:

Believe it or not, there are some who would rather snuggle with a werewolf (if there were such a thing) than get close to a good joke! Gelotophobia is a term that describes strong, negative feelings that are triggered by the sound of laughter. People who suffer from gelotophobia are afraid that people are really laughing at them.

Q Why did the flesh-eating monster spit out the clown?

A Because he tasted funny.

RIDDLE ME THIS

A riddle is a joke that sounds like a puzzle. Riddles usually ask questions that have clever or tricky answers. Many riddles use puns. Here's an example:

> Why is the longest nose on a monster only 11 inches?

> Because if it was twelve inches, it would be a foot.

Get it? If you do, then you know that one foot is 12 inches. Of course, the riddle doesn't work when translated to metric measurement. Riddles aren't usually fall-down-laughing funny, but there is enjoyment in solving the puzzle.

Q What do you do with a green monster?

A Wait until it ripens.

GRUNT AND SNARL

Monster humor often uses funny descriptions to get a chuckle. The exaggerated characteristics of monsters, such as horns, jagged teeth, and large, googly eyes are funny because we know they are make-believe. Sometimes, just making monster-like grunts and snarls is enough to make others laugh. That's because they are designed to be louder and wackier to attract attention.

Sir Monty Slugoslime

Whoopletootsie, Agent of Doom

Flubberphart

Q How can you tell which end of a worm is the head?

A Tickle it in the middle and see which end laughs!

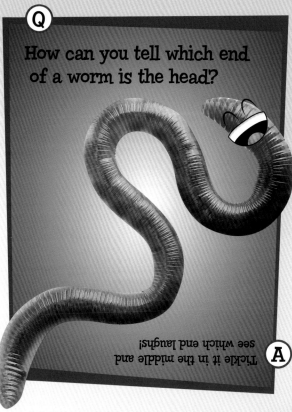

SIMILES

A simile is a comparison of two things using the words "like" or "as." Similes can be funny, especially when they compare two things that are not alike. Some similes have been around such a long time that they are no longer funny. Similes tend to be the most funny when we haven't heard them before, or when the comparison is so surprising or shocking that it makes us burst out laughing. "Crazy like a fox" is an old familiar simile, but "As smelly as King Kong's armpits" might crack you up!

FUNNY BONE:

Schadenfreude is a German term that means "harm-joy." It is used to describe laughing at someone else's misfortune. It might sound mean, but Schadenfreude is harmless. Sometimes, people even use Schadenfreude as a way to cope in difficult times. Seeing the dark humor in other people's problems can sometimes help us feel a lot better about our own struggles.

Chapter 4
Wordplay

Have you ever wondered why some people make us laugh more easily than others? In some cases, this might be because of the way they use words. The next time your favorite funny person gets you giggling, listen closely to the words you hear. You might be surprised to learn tricks that you can add to your own act.

METAPHORS

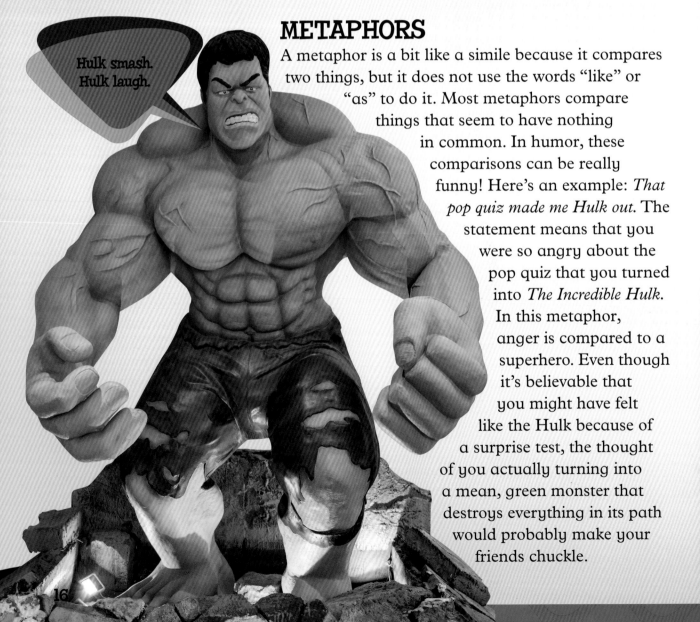

Hulk smash. Hulk laugh.

A metaphor is a bit like a simile because it compares two things, but it does not use the words "like" or "as" to do it. Most metaphors compare things that seem to have nothing in common. In humor, these comparisons can be really funny! Here's an example: *That pop quiz made me Hulk out.* The statement means that you were so angry about the pop quiz that you turned into *The Incredible Hulk*. In this metaphor, anger is compared to a superhero. Even though it's believable that you might have felt like the Hulk because of a surprise test, the thought of you actually turning into a mean, green monster that destroys everything in its path would probably make your friends chuckle.

GOT AN ITCH IN MY CATTYWAMPUS

Ever laughed really hard and not known why? Humor has a lot to do with the words you use. That's because some words are made to tickle our funny bone. They just sound funny. Just think about these words: frizzle, bumfuzzle, cattywampus, and nostril. Giggling yet? How about ogre, ghoul, shrivel, festering, and gelatinous? These words give us the creeps, because of another word: **onomatopoeia**. Try saying that three times fast! Onomatopoeia is a term that describes words that sound like their meaning. Think slithering, scaly, or puke. Grossed out? See if you can make your pals crack up when you use some of these shivery-shuddery words.

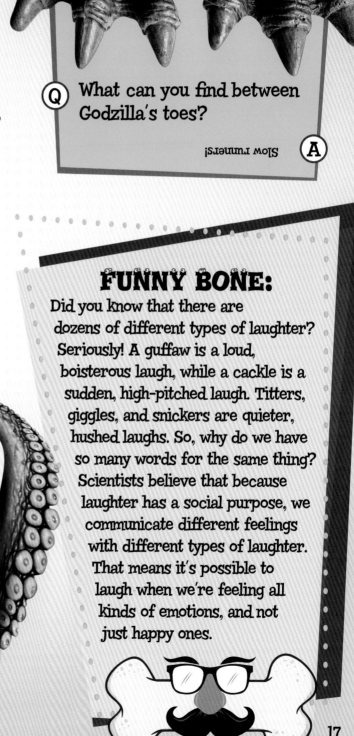

Q What can you find between Godzilla's toes?

A Slow runners!

ONOMATOPOEIA:
words that sound like their meaning, such as bam, bang, slam, gurgle, whizz, whoosh, or belch.

FUNNY BONE:
Did you know that there are dozens of different types of laughter? Seriously! A guffaw is a loud, boisterous laugh, while a cackle is a sudden, high-pitched laugh. Titters, giggles, and snickers are quieter, hushed laughs. So, why do we have so many words for the same thing? Scientists believe that because laughter has a social purpose, we communicate different feelings with different types of laughter. That means it's possible to laugh when we're feeling all kinds of emotions, and not just happy ones.

IT FIGURES

An **idiom** is a funny word for an expression that has both **figurative** and **literal** meanings. Figurative meanings have more to do with how words sound than what they actually mean. Literal meanings are exactly what the words say. Confused? Take the idiom "dead as a doornail." It means dead or lifeless, sure, but can a doornail be anything other than that? Of course not. That's where the literal meaning comes in. Idioms make everyday speech more colorful.

Idioms are often specific to cultures. They are used so commonly that they do not need explaining, unless you are talking to someone who is new to your country. Ever heard of the green-eyed monster? That's an idiom that describes someone who is so jealous (green) that they show their bad side, or turn into a monster.

What do you think? Clear as mud?

Q What does the invisible man drink with his cookies?

A Evaporated milk.

18

THAT'SSS SSOOO SSILLY

Alliteration is a trick of the tongue that combines the same first letters in a string of words. For example:

Seven saucy sorcerers scared sixteen slithering silverfish silly.

Q

Why wouldn't they let the butterfly into the dance?

Because it was a mothball.

A

Alliteration can be really funny, and also really clever! It's a great tool for showing off your vocabulary. With plenty of practice, you can use alliteration to liven up your jokes and get your friends giggling.

FUNNY BONE:

Homophones are commonly used in humor writing. That's because they so easily trip people up. A homophone is a word that sounds like another word, such as be and bee, might and mite, or scull and skull. Saying, "Keisha found the scull by the lake" has a different meaning than "Keisha found the skull by the lake." In the first statement, Keisha found a type of rowing boat, and in the second, she found a skeleton of a human or animal head!

Chapter 5
Monsterous Beasts and Unscary Bugs

Gags and physical comedy are common to monster and creepy-crawly humor. Other tricks that can be used to get a laugh are language and special types of speech. Let's take a closer look at some of them.

DON'T BE SCARED OF SYNONYMS

A synonym is something that is very similar to something else. For example, "frightening" is a synonym of "scary." Also, "funny" is a synonym of "hilarious" or "hysterical." Many comedians use synonyms in their acts, using words that we might not hear very often. Hearing a synonym makes our brains work harder, so when we "get it," there is a payoff. It is very similar to understanding the punch line of a joke.

Synonyms can be a fun and silly way to challenge your vocabulary. How many synonyms can you think of for the word "monster?" How about "beast," "villain," "behemoth," "devil," or "hellion?" How about the words you might use to describe the qualities of a monster? Think of characteristics such as foul breath, scraggly fur, slimy eyes, and claws.

Q What did the evil chicken lay?

A Deviled eggs.

Q
What does the headless horseman ride?

A
A night-mare!

ANTONYMS

An antonym is a word that is the opposite of another word. For example, "bad" is an antonym of "good," and "devil" is an antonym of "angel." Antonyms can be funny because they create contrasts. Sometimes antonyms surprise us, and that can be funny, too. Can you think of monster or creepy-crawly antonyms for these words?

- Smooth
- Hairy
- Foul
- Stinky
- Mean
- Sweet
- Kind

FUNNY BONE:
A malapropism is the use of an incorrect word with a word that sounds very similar. Malapropisms can be hilariously funny and are sometimes used to make people laugh. An example of a malapropism is: "the monster is just a pigment of your imagination." Here, pigment, which means color, is incorrectly used instead of figment, which means something that is not real.

21

VISUAL ANTONYMS

Have you ever noticed that sometimes monsters aren't
very clever? Think of the Abominable Snowman, who
thunders around the Arctic, but is too slow and dim-
witted to hurt anyone. With his soft white fur, he looks
more like an oversized teddy bear than a fearsome
monster. In animated movies, villains and monsters
are often given funny or silly characteristics, such as
moving slowly, to make them
seem less threatening.

Q

What does the Abominable Snowman
use frozen Band-aids for?

Cold Cuts.

A

Q

What do you get when
you cross a yeti with
a kangaroo?

A fur coat with pockets.

A

Q

What's a vampire's favorite fruit?

A Neck-tarines.

Q

Where do spirits buy their food?

A At the ghost-ery store.

FUNNY BONE:

A blooper, or gag reel, is a short film or video of the hilarious mistakes made in television shows or movies. Bloopers are outtakes, or parts of the show or movie that were edited or taken out of the final version. Sometimes they show actors messing up their lines and laughing.

Chapter 6
Creepy Fun and Games

Spooky monster humor is different around the world. What is funny or scary to one culture may not be to another. Since humor and laughter are a big part of how we develop social bonds, it makes sense that the things that give us the willies and the giggles are part of what makes each culture unique.

GODZILLA

Godzilla is a huge, reptile-like monster in Japanese culture. Godzilla movies were first created after the bombings of Hiroshima and Nagasaki during **World War II**. The monster was a metaphor for the nuclear weapons that destroyed these cities and took so many lives. Godzilla's fiery **atomic** breath and scaly, scarred skin are characteristics that show the serious damage these weapons can cause. The Godzilla movies from the 1950s may look more funny than scary now because we're used to special effects that can make monsters look more lifelike in movies.

> **Q** What did Godzilla eat after his tooth was pulled?
>
> **A** The dentist.

Halloween is a popular holiday that takes place on October 31. At this time of year, some families like to play jokes on visitors with porch gags. Spooky recorded laughter that plays when the doorbell is rung, skulls in the mailbox, and spider webs across the doorway are just some of the many tricks that are meant to tease visitors.

MACABRE

Several people around the world celebrate the **macabre**, which is a word that describes things that are grim or death-like, but often funny, too. In North America, many people love to walk through haunted houses, where they scream and laugh. Midnight cemetery walks are also popular in North America and Europe.

Q

What runs around the cemetery but doesn't move?

A fence.

A

FUNNY BONE:

Deadpan is a word that describes comedy that is delivered without emotion. When a comic delivers a joke "deadpan," he or she sounds very bored. The contrast between the hilarious things the comic is saying and the lack of body language or expression on the comic's face can be hysterical to audiences.

WANT TO TRY A SPOOKY PRANK?

Here is an activity that you can use to scare your friends and family. But remember, not everyone likes to be scared, so pick your victims carefully!

FINGER IN A BOX

Supplies:
- Small cardboard box
- Chalk in different colors
- Cotton batting (enough to fill the box)
- Red food coloring
- Scissors

Step 1: Cut a hole in the bottom of the box. The hole should be large enough to stick your middle finger through.

Step 2: Slip your finger through the hole, while keeping the box in the palm of the same hand.

Step 3: Place the cotton around your finger to cover the hole in the box.

Step 4: Drip red food coloring onto the cotton so that it looks like blood.

Step 5: Draw on your finger with different colors of chalk, so that your finger looks damaged or cut off.

Step 6: Put the lid on the box. Hide it behind your back or in your coat or pants pocket.

Step 7: Tell your friends that you found a missing finger. Use synonyms, similes, or metaphors to explain how disgusting it is. Then say that you have the finger in a box in your pocket.

Step 8: When your friends ask to see the finger, pull out the box, slip your finger through the hole, and use your other hand to remove the lid.

Step 9: When your friends look more closely, wiggle your finger a bit. Mwuahhahaahahaaaaa!!!!

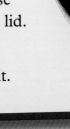

Q

What did the grandfather monster say to his grandson when they hadn't seen each other for quite awhile?

You gruesome!

A

Q

Why do werewolves have hairy coats?

Fur protection.

A

FUNNY BONE:

In many cultures that celebrate Christmas, Santa Claus brings gifts to well-behaved children every December. But in German folklore, Krampus visits the homes of families who live in the mountains, to scare and punish children who have misbehaved. Unlike jolly St. Nick, Krampus is a hairy beast with a tail, long tongue, and horns! Even though Krampus looks frightening, the tradition of Krampus is meant to be lighthearted and humorous.

Chapter 7
Your Guide to Funny

Making people laugh takes special talent, but there are many tricks of the trade that funny people use. Think you have what it takes to be a real funny person? Have some fun with these tips.

MAKING PROPS

When it comes to monster humor, props can be used to trick your audience into seeing things that aren't really there. Sometimes, the cheesier or sillier the prop, the better! You can easily make your own props. For example, ketchup, barbecue sauce, and red food coloring can be used to make fake blood. Costume and gag gift shops are also great places to find funny props, such as a fake hammer that you can use to whack your fingers. Or how about an arrow that can be worn as a headband, but looks like it goes right through your brain?

Q What kind of witch do you find in the fridge?

A A sandwich.

Q Why did the fly never land on the computer?

A He was afraid of the world wide web.

28

MAKING PEOPLE LAUGH

Making your friends laugh can be a lot different from yukking it up in front of an audience. Here are some tips that the pros use:

1. **Timing is everything.** Don't rush. When you race through your act, the audience might not pick up on everything that you say. Take your time, and speak loudly and clearly. Pause between jokes to give your audience a chance to laugh, and recover, before launching your next joke.

2. **Use body language and tone.** Moving your body in different ways can change the meaning of a joke. For example, covering your face in pretend embarrassment can give people the giggles. Try delivering a couple of jokes in deadpan.

3. **Choose your words carefully.** Use descriptive words. Try to use similes or metaphors.

4. **Pull a face.** Sometimes, just a twitch of the mouth can get people roaring. For monster humor, practice silent, screaming mouths and large, horrified eyes. Slap your hands on your cheeks and try a frightened expression. These are all ways of being funny by showing rather than telling.

5. **Practice makes perfect.** Rehearse your jokes in front of a mirror. Try using different voices, gestures, and body movements. Practice until you feel comfortable.

Q

Why didn't Dracula have any friends?

He was a pain in the neck.

A

FUNNY BONE:
Have you ever noticed how some comedians repeat a sentence more than once? This is known as a catchphrase, and it makes a comedian unique. Some catchphrases are so famous, people will laugh before the words are even out of the comedian's mouth!

Chapter 8
Find Out More

Want more funny? Here are some sources to help you learn more!

WEBSITES:

www.pbskids.org/halloween
A fun monster and Halloween games site.

www.kids.nationalgeographic.com/explore/halloween-hangout
Check out the Halloween hangout page for games, photos, and jokes.

BOOKS:

Leno, Jay. *How to Be the Funniest Kid in the Whole Wide World.* Simon & Schuster, 2005.

Rich, Susan and Various. *Half-Minute Horrors.* HarperCollins, 2011.

Szpirglas, Jeff. *Fear This Book: Your Guide to Fright, Horror, and Things That Go Bump in the Night.* Owlkids Books, 2006.

Hall of Humor

Bela Lugosi

Bela Lugosi was a Hungarian-American actor who became famous for playing Count Dracula and other creepy roles. He was a master of spooky acting, especially since his first roles were in silent films. He slicked back his hair and used white makeup on his face to look corpse-like. He also used horrified and serious facial expressions. In speaking roles, Lugosi delivered his lines in a deep, dramatic voice to haunt moviegoers.

Haunted Houses

Haunted houses can be scary, but fun. Visitors walk through rooms that are dimly lit or dark, and are scared by spooky music and sound effects. Sudden surprises, like monsters jumping out from behind curtains, or breathing close to visitors' faces, can send some running for home. Fog machines and gross smells are also used to create an atmosphere of horror.

FUNNY BONE:

Next Halloween, trick your friends by placing different gross things in bowls, then turning out the lights and asking them to tell you what they feel. You can use cold, cooked spaghetti for brains, peeled grapes for eyeballs, and Jell-O for witches' livers. Can you think of more?

Glossary

Note: Some boldfaced terms are defined where they appear in the text.

atomic Relating to nuclear energy, or describing a sudden, violent, and powerful blast

epidemic A sudden, widespread occurrence of a disease, or something that springs up suddenly

figurative Something that has a meaning different from the meaning of the actual or literal use of a word

idiom A form of expression

improv Comedy that is created for an audience on the spur of the moment, or without preparation or rehearsal

literal Stating facts as they really are

macabre Something that is disturbing or horrifying

parody An imitation of a particular person or style

pun When a word can have different, often humorous, meanings

punch line The final phrase or part of a joke, where the humor lies

setup The beginning of a joke or part of a story that "sets up" the humor

World War II A war that took place from 1939-1945 when the Allies (the United Kingdom and its former colonies and dominions, the Soviet Union, and the United States) defeated the Axis powers (Germany, Italy, and Japan)

Index